IN PROFILE

Leaders of the Russian Revolution

Fred Newman

SILVER BURDETT

In Profile

Women of the Air
Founders of Religions
Tyrants of the Twentieth Century
Leaders of the Russian Revolution
Pirates and Privateers
Great Press Barons
Explorers on the Nile
Women Prime Ministers
The Founders of America
The Cinema Greats
The War Poets
The First Men Round the World

First published in 1981 by
Wayland Publishers Ltd
49 Lansdowne Place, Hove
East Sussex BN3 1HF, England

© Copyright 1981 Wayland Publishers Ltd

Adapted and Published in the United States by
Silver Burdett Company, Morristown, N.J.

1982 Printing

ISBN 0-382-06632-4

Library of Congress Catalog Card No. 81-86278

Phototypeset by Direct Image, Hove, Sussex
Printed in the U.K. by Cripplegate Printing Co. Ltd.

Contents

Lenin	5
Lenin directs the struggle from abroad	9
The hero returns to the new order	14
Dates and events	19
Trotsky	21
Trotsky's criticism leads to his downfall	26
Trotsky flees from Stalin's assassins	32
Dates and events	35
Kerensky	37
Kerensky fails to stem Bolshevik challenge	44
Dates and events	49
Kornilov	51
German peace fuels Red Army's opposition	56
Dates and events	61
Glossary	62
Further reading	62
Index	63

Vladimir Ilyich Lenin

> Lenin grew up in a time when Russia was reacting to both the industrial and political changes of Europe. He learned much from the new revolutionary thinkers outside Russia, and their political beliefs became the sole driving force of this determined man. The tyranny of the Tsars must be smashed. Power must go to the workers and peasants. In reality, the new power, earned by the blood of many, gave birth to tyranny in a new form.

In the latter years of the nineteenth century, Russia was divided into the poor and the very rich—the landed nobles. Four out of every five Russians were peasants, living in conditions of extreme poverty. The nation was governed by Tsar Nicholas II, whose ancestors had ruled Russia for three hundred years. Into this world, on 20th April 1870 in a small town called Simbirsk, the wife of the local inspector of schools gave birth to a boy. That boy was Vladimir Ilyich Ulyanov, or, as he later became known, Lenin.

Throughout Lenin's childhood, Russia began slowly to experience those changes which had for more than half a century been altering the character of the more advanced European countries. Industrialization was creeping into agricultural Russia. So, too, were the political ideas bred in the changing societies of Europe. Although the Tsar's secret police sought to stamp out any opponents to his rule, they found it less easy to stamp out revolutionary thinking. An idea could not be thrust into prison; an idea could not be contained.

This new political thinking threatened the established systems of government and called for power to be transferred to the workers and the peasants.

As a young man, Lenin was exposed both to the new politics of revolution and to the forceful action

Tsar Nicholas II. His ancestors had ruled Russia for three hundred years, but in Lenin's youth, new political ideas were threatening the power of the royal house.

taken by the police to stop these ideas reaching the Russian people. His brother was hanged for his revolutionary activities, and Lenin, who had been studying law at university, was himself expelled and imprisoned.

One of the works that greatly influenced Lenin's thinking was *Das Kapital*, by Karl Marx. It inspired him to do all he could to bring about a great revolution in his native Russia. He did, however, continue his legal studies privately and in his final exams finished top of 124 candidates.

Because of his political activities, he was closely watched by the police, but Lenin continued to preach his ideas and gradually became known in international revolutionary circles.

The battle of wits between him and the authorities took on all the aspects of a secret war. Lenin formed his colleagues into secret cells of six, none of whom knew each other's identity. Letters were written in invisible ink and codes were used to disguise real names.

Lenin travels abroad

In March 1895, Lenin caught pneumonia and went abroad to speed his recovery. He travelled to Switzerland, France and Germany, where he met other revolutionary leaders. Meanwhile in Russia, the campaign against the revolutionaries had been stepped up. Lenin's mother wrote to her son telling

On his travels through Europe, Lenin met several revolutionary leaders.

Much of Lenin's enthusiasm for revolution was fired by the writings of this man, Karl Marx.

him that there was 'no hurry' for him to return.

Lenin ignored the hint. More than that, he took back to Russia with him pamphlets and a small printing press hidden in a secret compartment of his trunk. Although this was not discovered, Lenin was soon in trouble with the authorities once more, and, this time, exiled to Siberia.

But events were now running in Lenin's favour. The explosive forces of revolution in Russia were building up. Lenin was convinced that it was only a question of time before the Tsar would be overthrown and the people would rise up against his rule.

Lenin directs the struggle from abroad

In nineteenth-century Russia, the population was divided into the rich land-owners and the extremely poor peasants.

Lenin works from Munich then London in an attempt to spread revolutionary propaganda... Brussels meeting of Social Democratic Party establishes Bolsheviks as a political force... 'Bloody Sunday' massacre in St. Petersburg... Strikes cease as Tsar reasserts authority... Great War protest forces setting up of Provisional Government under Kerensky.

Lenin thought it would be easier for him to bring about the revolution by working abroad. In Munich he published a newspaper called *Iskra* (*The Spark*), with the aim of spreading those ideas which would lead to revolution. It was under the articles he wrote in this paper that Vladimir first used the name of Lenin.

Before long, Lenin was forced to quit Germany, and in 1902 he went to London, where he took a flat

This 'mugshot' of Trotsky in his early twenties was kept by the Tsar's secret police in their files of dangerous revolutionaries.

near King's Cross Station.

The international socialist movement was growing with every month that passed. But, as it grew, so did the disagreements between its various leaders.

Lenin himself believed that the party leaders should be composed only of professional revolutionaries. These men would lay down party policies and ordinary party members would have no right to vote. It was a belief which few of Lenin's colleagues held, but his fierce arguments eventually won the day, although they lost him friends.

In 1902, these issues were debated, often angrily, at a meeting of the Social Democratic Party held in a warehouse in Brussels. The outcome was a deep split in the revolutionary movement. Lenin and his supporters were in the majority and called themselves Bolsheviks, which means majority. Trotsky, Lenin's old friend, and others who opposed Lenin became known as Mensheviks—the minority.

'Bloody Sunday'

These differences, bitter though they were, did not discourage the spread of discontent within Russia itself. That great nation was slipping relentlessly towards violence and civil war.

Russia had become involved in war with Japan in 1904, but it was not a struggle for which the Russian people had any heart. A year later, in January 1905, a crowd of 200,000 workers marched to the Tsar's Winter Palace in St. Petersburg to petition for better conditions.

Though the march was a peaceful one, the authorities were nervous and over-reacted. Police and soldiers opened fire on the crowds. When Lenin learned of the massacre—it came to be called 'Bloody Sunday'—his first emotion was one of joy. This, he thought, would signal the beginning of the end for the Tsar and his order.

Police and soldiers fired on the crowds who were peacefully petitioning the Tsar for better conditions. This massacre soon became known as 'Bloody Sunday'.

Peasants attacked their landlords, and workers in other towns and cities joined their comrades in St. Petersburg in strikes and demonstrations. Lenin, in the room in Geneva where he was staying at the time, eagerly awaited each day's news of the breakdown of law and order. These were the conditions that heralded the revolution.

The Tsar reasserts his authority

Yet Lenin did not return to Russia immediately. By the time he did, some months later that autumn, the Tsar had become more and more alarmed by the outbreaks of protest and violence. In an attempt to calm the situation, he set up an elected parliament—the Duma—and extended a pardon to all political exiles.

Propaganda was one of the most powerful weapons in the armoury of the revolutionaries. This painting shows Lenin receiving the first propaganda leaflet off the printing press.

Worse still, from Lenin's point of view, the initiative had been taken by his rivals, the Mensheviks, who claimed to be the true revolutionaries. But in the event, neither they, nor Lenin's Bolsheviks were able to make any political impact.

Gradually, the strikes faded out and the Tsar began to reassert his authority. He punished both the workers who had led the strikes and the peasants who had risen in the countryside.

Had the revolution failed? A good many thought so, but not Lenin. He blamed the Mensheviks for lack of militancy, and decided that revolution would succeed only if he could lead his own party. Lenin felt there was little point in trying to bring the Mensheviks around to his own views. They would simply have to be ignored.

In 1912, he called a Social Democratic Party conference in Prague, taking care to invite only his followers. The Mensheviks were excluded and Lenin announced that only the Bolsheviks represented the Russian workers.

Naturally, the Mensheviks were furious. But Lenin had won an important propaganda victory. The conference called for armed revolt and an eight-hour working day for Russian workers. These demands proved appealing to the people of Russia and many joined the Bolshevik party. But Lenin's efforts to speed the revolution by smuggling arms into the country were not very successful.

A provisional government

What, in fact, brought the revolution to a head was an event over which Lenin had no control. In 1914, the Great War broke out in Europe. The enormous losses suffered by the Russian army together with shortages of food and the obvious inability of the Tsar to direct the war effort combined to drive the Russian people to revolt.

In February 1917, more than 200,000 workers came out on strike in St. Petersburg. When the Tsar ordered his troops to use force against the strikers, they refused. After 300 years of rule, the authority of the Tsars had finally broken down. Nicholas II had no option but to renounce his powers. A provisional government now ruled a Russia in which the workers were at least represented.

This scene of Russian troops leading a column of German prisoners of war was not a typical one.

The hero returns to the new order

Lenin returns to Russia to a hero's welcome... He is soon forced to flee to Finland... Bolsheviks take Petrograd; Lenin returns... He is elected President of People's Commissars... Lenin dismisses minority parliament: deputies driven out at gunpoint... Bolsheviks make peace with Germany... Lenin leaves legacy of new tyranny.

Lenin was in Switzerland when these historic events took place, and he could scarcely wait to join the revolution that had now clearly begun. But how? Germany and Russia were at war and there seemed no way he could reach St. Petersburg.

Happily, the interests of Germany came to his aid. On the afternoon of 9th April 1917, Lenin boarded a train that was to take him in greatest secrecy from Switzerland to Russia. The train had been provided by Germany. Why should the Germans have gone to such lengths to transport this Russian back to his own country? And why in a train that was carefully sealed so that its occupants should have no contact with anyone outside?

Lenin returns to Russia

Lenin believed that the war between England, France and Russia on the one side and Germany and Austria on the other was merely a struggle between capitalist powers. It had little to do with the interests of the Russian people.

In Lenin's view, the Russian people should stop fighting against Germany and direct their efforts instead to overthrowing the Tsar and his government. The German leaders were well aware of Lenin's views. He had preached them constantly through underground newspapers and pamphlets. They believed it was in their interest to transport Lenin across Germany so that he could return to Russia and spread his ideas among the Russian people. If any one man could get Russia out of the war, leaving Germany free to battle only against the Western allies, that man was Lenin.

As Lenin sat in his enclosed train, he had no idea how he would be received on his arrival in Russia.

After crossing by ferry from Germany to Sweden, and another train journey to St. Petersburg, Lenin realized that he had returned home to a hero's welcome. The excited shouts and cheers of the huge crowd; the band playing the revolutionary marseillaise; the red banners—this was evidence enough.

Throughout his career, Lenin had believed that the end justified the means—any action needed to put his ideas into practice was acceptable. He now said that the Provisional Government must be overthrown, that the landlords should be deprived of their estates and that Russia must withdraw from the war.

Once again, his fiery determination overcame his opponents. It seemed to Lenin that it would be only a matter of time before the Provisional Government collapsed and he would take power. In fact, after a final and hopeless onslaught against the Germans that year and a number of riots, the struggle between the Provisional Government and the revolutionaries reached its climax.

The government had sought to blame the Bolsheviks for their troubles, and ordered Lenin's arrest. Lenin went into hiding for some weeks. By November 1917, he had sought refuge in Finland. But in St. Petersburg, or Petrograd as it was now called, the government continued its desperate campaign against the revolutionaries.

Lenin takes control

Lenin had returned to a hero's welcome. He was now sure that the Provisional Govenment would fall and power would be his.

The Bolshevik headquarters in Petrograd were situated in a former girls' school, Smolny Convent. Its telephone wires were cut, and elsewhere the offices of the Bolshevik newspaper, *Rabochy Put (Workers' Path)*, were ransacked.

When the Provisional Government attacked the Bolsheviks' headquarters, Trotsky ordered his men to defend the building by force.

Lenin's old friend, Trotsky, with whom he had largely settled his political differences, reacted swiftly. Trotsky was at the Convent, and he ordered the Bolsheviks to defend their headquarters by force.

By the morning of 6th November, the revolutionaries were in control of all the key points in the city. They had met with no resistance, and Lenin, who had reached the city in disguise, issued a victorious proclamation.

Now Lenin showed how ruthless he could be in the pursuit of his aims. He had no time for the more moderate attitudes of the Mensheviks. By now his opponents realized that they would not be given any share in the new-found communist power.

Lenin called once more for an end to the war and for an end to private ownership. His words were received with enthusiasm, and Lenin was elected President of the Soviet of People's Commissars.

A new tyranny

Having won power, Lenin lost no time in ensuring that he should keep it. He had struggled against the tyranny of the Tsar and the ruthlessness of the secret police. Now he began to impose his own tyranny and to set up his own police force in the name of the new 'socialist democracy'.

Although he had agreed to the holding of elections, he did not allow the parties who opposed the Bolsheviks to hold political meetings. Despite this advantage, the Bolsheviks failed to gain a majority in the new parliament. Lenin's swift answer was to dissolve it, and its deputies were driven out at gunpoint.

In 1918, Lenin signed a peace treaty with Germany, despite the opposition of many of his colleagues. The treaty gave away huge areas of territory to the Germans. This made the Bolsheviks unpopular in Russia. So did the use of force to carry out land reforms and to maintain discipline in the factories.

Violence bred more violence, both by the Bolsheviks and by their enemies in Russia. On

Little more than a year after this photograph was taken of Lenin presiding over a meeting of the Council of People's Commissars, Russia's leader was to die.

16th July 1918, it is believed that Lenin's secret police murdered Tsar Nicholas II and all his children and servants.

Then, just over a month later, on 30th August, Lenin himself was shot after a meeting in Moscow at which he had addressed the local workers. Lenin recovered from his wounds, but he was never able to build the kind of Russia he had once envisaged. The true socialist democracy was never to be. Instead, there grew up a huge communist bureaucracy which even Lenin himself could not control.

When Lenin died in January 1924, after a long illness, he left a Russia very different to the one into which he had been born over fifty years earlier. The ancient rulers had been swept away, as had some, but not all, of the poverty of the peasants. But the absolute dictatorship of the Tsars had simply been replaced by another equally undemocratic regime upon which the ordinary Russian had little, if any, influence.

Dates and events

1870	Vladimir Ilyich Ulyanov (Lenin) is born.
1887	Lenin's brother is hanged.
1891	Lenin qualifies as a lawyer.
1895	Lenin is arrested and imprisoned.
1897	Lenin is exiled to Siberia.
1898	First Congress of the Russian Social Democratic Party is held. Lenin marries Nadezhda Krupskaya.
1900	Lenin leaves Siberia and returns to European Russia. The first issue of *Iskra* appears.
1903	Lenin resigns from *Iskra*.
1904	Outbreak of war between Russia and Japan.
1905	'Bloody Sunday'. Lenin returns from Switzerland to St. Petersburg.
1906	Russia's first elected parliament.
1914	The Great War is declared.
1917	The February Revolution begins. Germans aid Lenin's return from Switzerland in sealed train. Provisional Government orders raids on Bolshevik headquarters. Lenin dismisses elected parliament at gunpoint. Russia signs peace treaty with Germany. Great War ends.
1921	New Economic Policy is introduced.
1922	Lenin suffers first stroke.
1924	Lenin dies.

Leon Trotsky

> Trotsky was the romantic visionary of the revolution. He alone spoke out against the failures of the new socialist order at a time when Stalin was ruthlessly crushing any criticism of his regime. But, even in exile, he could not escape the vengeance of Russia's dictator. Twenty-three years after the birth of the communist state he had dreamed of, Trotsky's violent death merely confirmed that the dream had for long been a nightmare.

Like Lenin, Trotsky was forced to live and work in exile for periods in his life. Born Leon Davidovitch, he went to school in Odessa, and was soon involved in politics. He founded the South Russian Workers' Union, and his activities made him a target for the Tsar's secret police. He was imprisoned, escaped, and fled to Europe.

On one occasion, he met Lenin when they were both in London. But when, in 1917, news came of the Tsar's fall, Trotsky was in New York.

Revolutionaries like Trotsky were regarded with suspicion by governments everywhere. When Trotsky arrived in Nova Scotia en route for Russia, he was arrested by the British. Eventually he was released and allowed to continue his journey.

When he arrived in Russia, the country was on the verge of civil war. With the rule of the Tsars overthrown, the Bolsheviks were about to take over power. But they were still opposed by most of Russia's old guard—generals, landlords and church leaders.

It was Trotsky more than any other man who rallied the forces of the communists and organized the war against their Russian enemies. Trotsky's battle headquarters was a train which steamed along the fronts. From it, the small, dark-haired Trotsky, his pince-nez firmly fixed on his nose, issued orders to what was to become in the months ahead the mighty force known as the Red Army.

Trotsky's ruthless methods

Not only did Trotsky's train carry arms and ammunition for the troops; on board was a mobile telephone exchange, a library, and a printing press for the production of pamphlets.

The war was one of words as well as bullets. What was being fought over was not merely *who* should

In Lenin's absence, Trotsky ordered the Bolshevik troops to defend Smolny Convent by force.

Trotsky's special train carried arms and ammunition as well as a printing press for the production of propaganda pamphlets.

rule Russia, but *how* that vast and backward nation should be ruled. Trotsky, although he had had his differences with Lenin and the Bolsheviks from time to time, now worked energetically for their common victory.

While he was later to regret the way that the revolution had turned out, in those early days—and in 1918 he was still a relatively young man of 39—Trotsky still dreamed of a society whose wealth would be shared and controlled by its workers.

He was prepared to fight—to the death, if necessary—for such a dream. A visionary he may have been, but Trotsky could be as hard and ruthless as any man in the pursuit of his aims. He ordered deserters to be shot, and, though he stood for the workers, he had few scruples in having them killed when necessary. At one time during the uprising, mobs had stormed the cellars of a number of palaces. Trotsky ordered the Red Guards to hurl grenades on the crowds below.

Trotsky lived in his train for two and a half years. During this time, he travelled 160,000 kilometres. Once, when the train itself came under attack, he ordered the cooks and wireless operators to take up rifles to defend it. By the time the civil war was over, the Red Army had grown from 200,000 men to more than 5 million. Trotsky had been its architect.

The new order

Trotsky's views did not always agree with Lenin's. When Lenin dismissed the first 'democratic assembly', Trotsky had serious misgivings.

But he later had a change of heart—or he may simply have decided that he could be more useful to the revolution by working with the Bolsheviks. Whatever the case, it seemed to Trotsky that the movement toward great social and industrial change in Russia had taken a great step forward with the victory of the communists.

True, there was still rebellion and unrest in parts of the country. It seemed to him, though, that the foundations could now be laid for the kind of society that would improve the lot of the Russian people. This new order would bring to them some of the material advantages that workers in the more

Trotsky had increased the numbers of the Red Army to more than 5 million by the time the civil war was over.

Trotsky listened as Lenin spoke to soldiers before they left for the Polish front.

industrially-advanced nations were beginning to enjoy.

Neither Trotsky nor Lenin believed in votes for every Russian, whatever his or her political beliefs. But, of the two, Trotsky was less of a dictator. If he had gained control of the communist party after the civil war, he might have made it less tyrannical than it turned out to be.

By 1922, although Lenin's health was failing and many saw Trotsky as his natural successor, a new contender for power had arrived on the Russian political scene.

Trotsky's criticism leads to his downfall

Stalin assumes power . . . Trotsky criticizes the failures of the revolution and attacks party leaders . . . He is expelled from the communist party . . . Stalin exiles Trotsky to Alma Ata . . . From there he goes to Constantinople . . . Stalin's show trials begin . . . Trotsky is sentenced to death . . . He flees Norway to avoid Stalin's agents . . . Arrangements are made for his exile in Mexico.

The man Lenin appointed to be general secretary of the Bolshevik party was called Joseph Stalin, a man much more ruthless in destroying his opponents than any who had gone before him.

Through his position, Stalin was able to control both the party machine and, of equal importance, the Press. He was also able to command the secret police, a force as cruel as the one that had once been used in the service of the Tsar. The revolution had replaced one tyranny with another!

Trotsky becomes isolated

To Stalin, Trotsky was a threat. First, Trotsky urged a policy of building up the factories. But Stalin believed technology would be wasted on Russia's peasant majority. Second, Trotsky was a hero in the eyes of many Russians for the role he had played in the civil war. And third, Stalin never trusted Trotsky, recalling that he had not always been on the side of the Bolsheviks.

While Trotsky was speaking out about some of the revolution's failures—for instance, peasants were having to pay three times as much for manufactured goods in 1923 as in 1917 and there were many shortages—Stalin was deliberately having Trostky's friends and allies sent to posts abroad.

Trotsky did not help his own cause by making an unwise attack on two party leaders, Zinoviev and Kamenev. This resulted only in losing him their support to Stalin.

Gradually, Trotsky was being isolated. He complained bitterly about the lies and half-truths that appeared about him in the newspapers. The break between him and the other Russian leaders grew larger month by month until, in 1927, he was expelled from the communist party. Soon after came the order for his exile to a remote part of Russia.

Yet to many Russian workers, Trotsky was still a

Trotsky, here with his staff, was the obvious choice as successor to Lenin. When the time came, however, power was handed to a much more ruthless man, Joseph Stalin.

romantic figure, to be admired as a true leader of the revolution and as one who represented their interests. Even the secret police officer who came to arrest him is supposed to have said: 'Shoot me, comrade Trotsky'. When the train taking Trotsky into exile began to pull out of Moscow, hundreds of workers blocked the line to prevent its departure. But the Soviet authorities were determined to get him out of the way. Trotsky was an embarrassment, and, the very next day, he and his wife were dragged to the station and put aboard another train.

For some time, Trotsky lived in the remote town of

Alma Ata. In those days it had no electric light, and was ridden by malaria, but Trotsky still managed to receive news from Moscow. In 1929, he was ordered to be deported. After a long journey by sledge and train across the frozen wastes of Russia, he was brought to Odessa.

At dead of night a ship called the *Ilyich*—Lenin's original name—sailed with Trotsky and members of his family and some friends to exile in Constantinople. These were fretful and frustrating years for Trotsky. His great visions of the future had been sadly shattered by the acts of a brutal regime. For the communist government had become as harsh as those in capitalist states, against which Trotsky had

Trotsky addresses a crowd in Red Square. The Russian people had always seen in Trotsky those romantic qualities which many revolutionaries lacked.

The peasants in this propaganda poster trample underfoot the relics of an imperial past.

Trotsky knew that his dreams of a new Russia had in reality become a nightmare. Here, inmates of a labour camp are put to constructing the Stalin-Belomor Canal.

campaigned for so many years.

Trotsky felt badly let down by what was happening in Russia. But there, in the Kremlin, it was Stalin who was trying to brand Trotsky a traitor. In 1932, the Russian rulers stripped him of his Russian nationality, but, even in exile, Trotsky was defiant.

He travelled from Constantinople through Europe, meeting other revolutionaries and defending himself against the many attacks that were being made on him by Stalin.

Meanwhile, terrible events were taking place in Russia. There was not enough food; many workers were starving; and opponents of Stalin were being killed by the secret police. Others were sent to

Stalin is seen here with Sergei Kirov, who in 1934 was to lead the growing opposition to Stalin's ruthless regime.

remote labour camps where they were made to dig canals and build roads.

Stalin staged spectacular trials. Most of the evidence produced by the State was made up, and Trotsky's name was mentioned on many occasions. He was accused of plotting against the regime, and even of assassinating some Russian leaders.

Finally, Trotsky was sentenced to death. It was certain that Stalin's agents would soon attempt to carry out the sentence—wherever Trotsky lived.

At that time, he was in Norway. Russia told the Norwegians that, if Trotsky was allowed to stay in Norway, it would cause trouble. Understandably, the Norwegians had no wish to upset their much more powerful neighbours. Even though they sympathized with Trotsky, the Russian was asked to leave.

Where could he go? What nation would offer him a haven? Eventually, arrangements were made for him to travel to Mexico, but Trotsky knew that he would probably not be safe there.

Trotsky flees from Stalin's assassins

Trotsky seeks refuge in Mexico... Both his sons die in suspicious circumstances... Trotsky is forced to live in seclusion, guarded by Mexican police... The first attempt on Trotsky's life fails... He is attacked by Jacson Mornard, supposedly a friend... His condition is not considered serious, but he goes into coma and soon after dies... His passing goes almost unnoticed.

The net was beginning to close around him. Within a short time he heard news that both his sons had died. The first was Sergey Sedov, aged 28, who was an engineer and not at all interested in politics. Sergey was shot after an accident in the Russian factory where he was working. The authorities blamed him for the accident, which, they said, had caused many workers to be gassed.

Trotsky, however, did not believe this story. He thought Sergey had been shot because of his father's political views. Soon afterwards, his other son, Leon

Trotsky arrives with his wife in Mexico.

Sedov, wrote to him from Paris saying that he was being followed by agents of the Russian secret police.

He, too, was soon dead—following an appendix operation from which he seemed to have recovered. Trotsky was convinced that, as before, his son's death was not an accident.

It was only a matter of time, Trotsky knew, before an attempt would be made to kill him. He lived in a house in Mexico that was quite on its own. It was surrounded by a high wall and its solid iron gate was guarded night and day by trusted colleagues. All visitors were examined through a spy-hole before the gate was opened.

Assassination attempts

Trotsky rarely went out; most of his time was spent in his study where, surrounded by the red-bound works of Lenin, he worked most of the time. Outside the house, the Mexican authorities had arranged for a police guard. The Russian exile seemed as safe as he could be.

But one night in May 1940, Trotsky was aroused by the sound of gun-fire. It sounded as if a machine-gun was being fired in the room next door. Trotsky and his wife crouched down below their bed.

In the next instant, the door burst open and bullets riddled the room. Somehow neither Trotsky nor his wife were hit, even though some sixty bullets had sprayed around the room.

The attempt had failed, but a few weeks later there came another. Among friends who were allowed to come and go freely, was a man called Jacson Mornard. Trotsky knew very little about Mornard, but this man had claimed to be an admirer of Trotsky and opposed to Stalin. He also had other friends in common with Trotsky.

On 20th August Mornard arrived at the house to show Trotsky an article he had written. Together they went into the study. Suddenly the door opened and Trotsky staggered out, his face covered in blood.

Apparently, while Trotsky and Mornard had been looking at the article, the visitor had pulled an ice-pick from under the raincoat he was wearing. There was a fierce struggle and, although Trotsky resisted his attacker, he was stabbed in the head by the ice-pick.

At first it seemed the wound was not too serious. At the hospital, the doctors were hopeful that Trotsky's life could be saved. But he fell into a coma, and died the next day.

Trotsky was sixty years old, and had become just another victim of Stalin's secret police force. No direct connection between Mornard and the Russians was ever proved, but it seemed the obvious explanation for the crime.

The world did not take much notice of the death in Mexico of Leon Trotsky. In Europe, much more dramatic events were happening. The Second World War had begun, and the RAF was fighting 'The Battle of Britain' against Hitler's Luftwaffe.

The murder of a tired old man who no longer had any hope of seeing his dreams come true was, in August 1940, hardly headline news.

Mexican police officers examine the ice-pick with which Trotsky was murdered.

This photograph of Trotsky was taken shortly before his assassination.

Dates and events

1879   Trotsky is born in Yanovka in the Ukraine.
1898   Trotsky is arrested as member of Marxist group and sent to Siberia.
1902   He escapes and joins Lenin in London.
1905   Trotsky is made president of the first Soviet in St. Petersburg.
1917   Fall of the Tsar. Trotsky returns from New York to Russia. He joins the Bolshevik party and, with Lenin, organizes the November Revolution. Disagreement over Lenin's dismissal of elected parliament.
1922   Lenin suffers his first stroke. He appoints Joseph Stalin general secretary to the Central Committee.
1924   Lenin dies. Trotsky's influence starts to decline.
1926   Stalin dismisses Trotsky from the Politbureau.
1927   Trotsky is exiled to Central Asia.
1929   Trotsky is deported from Russia to Constantinople.
1932   He is deprived of his Russian nationality.
1937   Trotsky is sentenced to death in his absence by a Russian court. He flees to Mexico.
1940   Trotsky is killed by Jacson Mornard. His passing goes almost unnoticed.

Alexander Kerensky

> Kerensky had been the only socialist in the Tsar's government. When the Provisional Government came to power, he was chosen as Prime Minister. But power was his in name alone. His attempts to stem the rising tide of the Bolshevik movement met with no success. Finally, when Kerensky was still in office, Trotsky ordered his arrest. He fled Russia and left his country to fight out a bloody civil war.

By a strange coincidence, Kerensky was born and raised in the village of Simbirsk, which was also Lenin's home town. In fact, Kerensky's father, the headmaster of the local school, had had young Lenin as one of his pupils!

Kerensky was not like Lenin or Trotsky, who both had very clear ideas on how Russia should be governed, but owed his advance to the fact that he was the only 'socialist' in the Tsar's government. So, when the new Provisional Government was set up after the Tsar was overthrown, Kerensky accepted the post of Minister of Justice.

But the Provisional Government did not really have the support of most of the Russian people. They were mainly unhappy with the way the government was conducting the war. Most of the Russian troops had no heart for it, and the Bolsheviks encouraged this unrest.

There were many demonstrations against the war and, to counter the effect of these, Kerensky was given the job of Minister of War. Kerensky believed in the war and wanted to keep Russian soldiers fighting. He went to the front to encourage them, and in June 1917 he ordered a big attack to be launched on the invading German army.

After one or two small victories, the Russian

As Minister of War, Kerensky had to encourage the Russian people as well as the Russian army to sustain the war effort.

soldiers suffered a huge defeat. Some 40,000 were killed, and the troops turned on their officers, murdering many of them, before retreating from the front.

What was Kerensky going to do now? His gamble had failed—in fact it never really had a chance of succeeding—and the government in which he found himself had very little real power.

Much more influence was exerted by the Soviet—the committee of workers in Petrograd which had been set up alongside the Provisional Government. So Russia really had *two* governments, and they did not even agree with each other.

Anti-government protests increase

All the time, more Soviets were being set up in other towns and the authority of the Provisional Government, never great, was becoming weaker and weaker.

Many Russian soldiers looked to the Soviet for their orders. Ordinary military discipline no longer applied in the Russian army. One of the new 'laws' issued by the Soviet—aimed to win the support of the soldiers—said that soldiers should organize their own committees to control weapons and that officers should be elected by the men themselves and must be 'polite' to their troops.

No wonder there was mutiny everywhere in the army! Inevitably, the German and Austrian armies continued their advances. As news arrived in

Bolshevik troops on the Galician front are seen here demonstrating against the war.

Kerensky (right) with Kornilov. At first united against the Bolsheviks, the two men soon became bitter opponents.

Petrograd of the heavy defeats at the front, mobs took to the streets to protest against the government.

Kerensky was able to get troops loyal to the government to restore order and on the 8th July he himself took over as Prime Minister. Kerensky feared that the Bolsheviks were plotting to take power. Although he had put down the riots, he had failed to take decisive action against the greater threat of Lenin and Trotsky.

The Bolsheviks wanted to see an end to the Provisional Government headed by Kerensky. On the other hand, there were many Russians who, although they no longer supported the Tsar and his rule, felt that the politics of the Bolsheviks were too extreme.

Kerensky stood somewhere in the middle. He had been chosen as Prime Minister simply because he was the least offensive to all sides. Unfortunately, Kerensky was not just a bumbler, he was a dreamer out of touch with what was going on around him.

Although he enjoyed the reputation of being a revolutionary, he was basically a man who took advantage of every situation. He enjoyed power. He liked addressing large meetings and often became quite hysterical while making speeches.

His main concern was still to keep Russia's army in the war. In this, he had the support of the Allies—the United States, Great Britain and France—who, of course, were also anxious that the German troops should continue to be engaged on the Russian front as well as in Europe.

Kerensky blames the Bolsheviks

Kerensky tried to put the blame for the defeats on the Bolsheviks who, he said, were German agents. Some of the Russian people believed this. It seemed to make sense, because everyone knew that the Bolsheviks were against the war. So, it would not be surprising if some of them were working for the Germans.

But Kerensky and his government were coming more and more under attack. Every day workers and soldiers were calling for the Soviet to take over all power and disband the Provisional Government altogether.

Armed Red Guards marched on the Tauride Palace in Petrograd where Kerensky had his headquarters.

The people were calling for the Soviet to take over from the Provisional Government, but still Kerensky clung to power.

In the streets, there was fighting between Cossacks, who supported the Provisional Government, and the Red Guards, who supported the Soviets.

The call for unity

Still Kerensky clung to power, and in August he called a 'State Conference' in Moscow—by that time Petrograd was too full of revolutionaries. The aim of the conference was to try to unite all the different elements in Russian society. Generals, soldiers, workers and peasants crowded into the hall. Only the Bolsheviks did not attend.

Kerensky delivered one of his most emotional speeches. He spoke of the need for unity and called upon everyone to support the Provisional Government. Attempts to overthrow it, he cried, would be 'put down with blood and iron'.

Many applauded these sentiments. Others were disappointed. They did not find the young Kerensky an impressive figure. One onlooker described him as 'a young man with a tortured, pale face and a pose like an actor speaking his lines'.

Even if Kerensky had been more persuasive, it is

doubtful whether his call for unity could have succeeded. Russia was already too deeply divided. As Kerensky occupied the stage, the elements of civil war were gathering in the wings. Right-wingers, left-wingers, Bolsheviks and liberals, loyalists and anarchists, all competed with each other for power.

Lenin was the leader of one of the many groups which were hoping to take over power from the fast-fading Provisional Government.

Kerensky fails to stem Bolshevik challenge

*The Bolsheviks gain in popularity . . .
Riga falls to the Germans . . .
Kerensky becomes more isolated . . .
He sends rebellious regiments to defend the front . . .
Petrograd taken by the Bolsheviks . . .
Trotsky announces fall of Provisional Government . . .
Resistance from officers and officials lacks army support . . .
Trotsky orders Kerensky's arrest . . .
Kerensky flees Russia.*

The situation in cities like Petrograd and Moscow was unreal. It was almost as if two Russias were leading separate existences side by side. The restaurants were open, and the rich continued to give parties and entertain their friends. The opera and ballet gave their performances as usual before enthusiastic audiences. But in the streets, red flags adorned the Tsarist monuments and fluttered from public buildings. Within the palaces various departments of the administration carried on, though outside it was not the police but the armed Red Guards who kept order.

The Bolsheviks grew steadily more popular. The people had forgotten the accusations made against them by Kerensky. They were much more concerned with the shortages and strikes. It also occurred to them that getting rid of Kerensky's government might help to solve Russia's problems.

Kerensky became more and more isolated. Few supported him, and the Soviet ruled in everything but name. By October, the city of Riga had fallen to the Germans and it seemed as if there was little to stop an advance on Petrograd itself.

Kerensky saw this as an opportunity to try to send the more rebellious regiments away from Petrograd

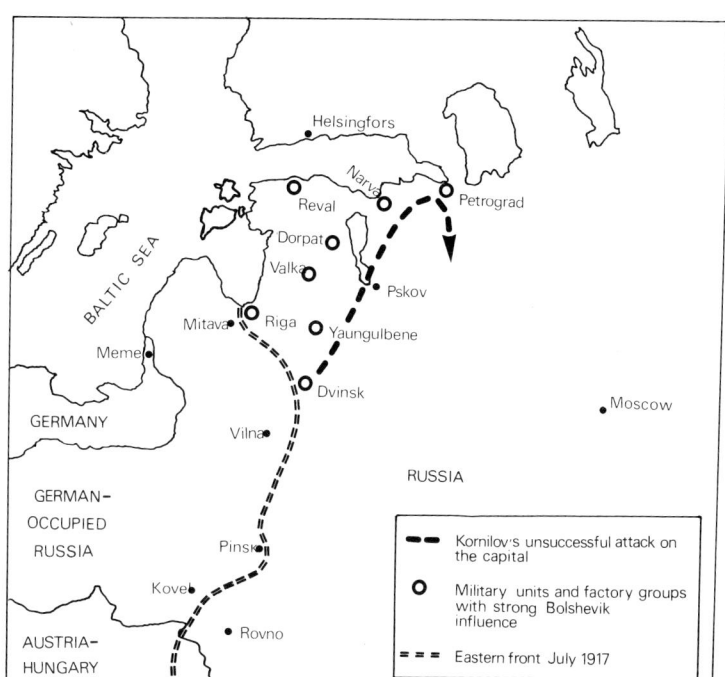

This map shows the main areas where opposition to the Provisional Government was centred.

Kerensky in Moscow after the State Conference which was held in the city in August 1917.

to defend the front. But by this time few in the armed forces were obeying the orders of the government.

The cruiser *Aurora*, many of whose crew were well known to be Bolshevik sympathizers, posed another threat to Kerensky. He gave orders for her to sail from her anchorage in Petrograd's River Neva. But Bolshevik workers lowered the bridges over the Neva and prevented her sailing.

Kerensky tried another desperate action against the Bolshevik threat. He attempted to close down the newspapers which they ran, but this, too, failed.

He next called for a vote of confidence in his government. While he spoke, the Bolsheviks were taking over! All over the city of Petrograd detachments of the Red Guards were seizing important buildings—the railway station, bridges, means of transport and communication, all passed into their control.

Kerensky knew that the only remaining hope of

In a final attempt to ward off the Bolshevik threat, Kerensky summoned to Petrograd those regiments loyal to the government.

countering the Bolsheviks was to summon regiments loyal to the Provisional Government to the city. He decided to call for help.

But how could he communicate with the commanders at the front? And how could he know which would support him against Lenin and Trotsky? There was only one way to be sure. He would have to slip out of the city and go to talk to the commanders himself. He commandeered a car from the American Embassy, and under the protection of their flag—

though Embassy officials themselves protested at his action—he managed to get through the barricades.

Meanwhile, in Petrograd ministers of Kerensky's government debated in the Malachite Chamber of the Winter Palace. There was little point to their discussions. There was nothing they could do. No one was left to carry out their commands. From their windows they could see the guns of the Russian fleet at anchor—and the guns were pointing at the Winter Palace.

Lenin assumes control

It was 7th November 1917. Trotsky had already announced that 'the Provisional Government has fallen'. That evening, shells began to fall on the Winter Palace.

No loyal troops marched to the government's rescue. Kerensky's journey to the front line was in vain.

None of the regiments he asked was prepared to march on Petrograd, and yet in the city itself there were still many who opposed the extreme ideas of the Bolsheviks. Though they were few in numbers, the Bolsheviks acted decisively under Lenin's leadership. They started to issue orders as though they *did* control the country.

There was resistance. Government employees and bank clerks went on strike. A group of officers even tried to storm the Petrograd telephone exchange, but after heavy fighting were beaten back by Red Guards.

Kerensky leaves Russia

Kerensky remained at the front, trying to arouse support for a battle with the Bolsheviks, and Trotsky issued orders for his arrest. The Prime Minister, realizing that the odds were now weighed heavily

When Kerensky realized that he had little chance of regaining power, he left Russia. Here he is seen in Paris.

against him, slipped quietly out of Russia.

It signalled the end of what little authority and power Kerensky had held during the extraordinary events of the past few months. He had clung obstinately to office long after it was clear that most of the Russian people had no faith in his government at all.

He spoke of uniting Russia, but he left it deeply divided. His determination to continue fighting the Germans in the end created sympathy for the Bolsheviks. All was confusion and uncertainty. True,

Kerensky left Russia in a state of confusion. Soon, as many had long feared, the country was to be plunged into civil war.

the army did not come to Kerensky's rescue. But what would happen now that he was gone? The worst fears of many—that the nation would be plunged into a terrible civil war—were soon to come about.

Dates and events

1881	Kerensky is born in the town of Simbirsk.
1898	First Congress of the Russian Social Democratic Party.
1904	Outbreak of war between Russia and Japan.
1905	Workers are massacred in 'Bloody Sunday' protest in St. Petersburg.
1906	Russia's first elected parliament.
1914	The Great War is declared.
1917	Kerensky is made minister of justice, then minister for war and finally prime minister. He is soon deposed by the Bolsheviks and flees to France.
1924	Lenin dies. Stalin comes to power.
1940	Kerensky goes to Australia.
1946	Kerensky goes to the United States.
1970	Kerensky dies.

Lavr Georgevitch Kornilov

> 'A lion's heart and brains of a sheep' —so Kornilov was described. To many less extreme Russians, Kornilov was the only man who could counter the threat of Bolshevik upheaval. But his efforts failed. Kornilov escaped arrest by Kerensky and fled south. Killed in action, this soldier did more than anyone to encourage the development of Trotsky's Red Army and thus to establish the power of the Bolsheviks.

The young officer peered through his field glasses at the fortifications of the Afghan army. Then, taking out his camera, he carefully photographed everything that might be useful to his own side, the Russians.

He was well behind the enemy lines, and, were he to be discovered, he knew all too well that it would mean certain death. But the officer, called Lavr Georgevitch Kornilov, gave no thought to such things. To him, all that mattered was carrying out a mission successfully.

This was the man who many years later was to lead a desperate war against the Bolsheviks. However many lives it cost, Kornilov was always convinced that he was right and that justice was on his side.

Kornilov was born into a military family—his father was an officer in a Cossack regiment—and he grew up in a Siberian garrison town. He was short and very dark-haired, with almost oriental eyes that gave him a Mongolian appearance.

His family were very poor, but by hard work and military studies in the cadet force, young Kornilov advanced his army career. Not being a member of the ruling classes in Russia, Kornilov had little loyalty for the Tsar, but he fought bravely for Russia.

Kornilov was no 'armchair general'. By 1917, when

the Tsar was overthrown, he was already something of a public hero. He had fought with distinction in the war against Japan, had served in China and then, at the start of the World War, commanded a brigade on the Carpathian front.

Kornilov was wounded and captured by the Austrians, but managed to make his escape and return to the Russian lines. These exploits and his sympathies for the revolutionaries made him a natural choice as a military leader.

However, Kornilov was not much interested in politics, and it was soon clear that he did not see eye to eye with Kerensky, the head of the Provisional Government.

'A lion's heart and brains of a sheep' was one comment made about Kornilov, and it is true that he was not very tactful or particularly clever in his dealings with the government.

As a soldier, Kornilov was appalled by the breakdown of military discipline in the army. The Soviet had abolished the death sentence, but Kornilov wanted it restored. He demanded that deserters from the army should be shot. He was angry and alarmed at the way the war against the Germans was going.

Kornilov felt sure that most of the army supported him, and it began to appear both to Kerensky and to

Kornilov soon made it clear that he did not support Kerensky and the Provisional Government, pictured here in 1917.

Kornilov's arrival at the State Conference gave many Russians the opportunity to express their support for his conservative policies.

the Bolsheviks that the general was himself plotting to take over power. When Kornilov arrived in Moscow in August 1917 for the State Conference that Kerensky had called, he was greeted by many as a saviour.

As Kornilov's train drew into the station, his personal bodyguards—members of the Tekintzy regiment—leapt onto the platform. Wearing long pink coats, they drew their curved swords and lined up on the platform in a guard of honour.

Kornilov loved this kind of ceremonial, and strode to his carriage amid the cheers of those who had gathered to witness his arrival. Flowers were thrown at his feet and ladies swooned. From the crowd came cries of 'Save Russia, Kornilov!'

The great man smiled and inclined his head. More and more he saw himself as the leader to stand against the Bolsheviks and gain a victory against the Germans.

Many Russians, too, who were conservative in their opinions, thought Kornilov was their only hope. Although he was not himself opposed to revolution, he became a hero to those who were.

Some 30,000 armed Bolshevik sailors marched into Petrograd to oppose Kornilov's attempt to take over the capital.

No wonder this rather simple man, who believed that everything could be solved by soldiers and with the use of force, began to get ideas of taking over power himself. He sent four of his best cavalry divisions to take up station near Petrograd, and in the month following the Conference in Moscow it looked as if Kornilov would make his attempt to take over the capital.

Kornilov's revolt fails

But Kornilov did not have as much support as he supposed. Many Russian workers were against him and his troops, and, before they could begin to march on Petrograd, their movements were sabotaged. The telegraph was disrupted and messages intercepted. Troop trains were shunted into sidings, trains diverted to the wrong destination, and tracks ripped up.

In Petrograd itself, the Red Guards manned defensive positions, but Kornilov's army never reached the city. Even the crack Savage Division, one of the most feared in Kornilov's command, was persuaded by messengers sent out from the Petrograd Soviet to renounce their leader. When the soldiers had listened to what the messengers had to say, they raised red banners on their vehicles, and arrested many of their officers!

Even during his imprisonment in a hotel room, Kornilov was allowed to take the salute while his regiments marched past outside.

Kornilov's revolt was a failure and within a short time Kerensky ordered his arrest. As we have seen, the Prime Minister had little power himself, and Kornilov's imprisonment was a strange affair.

The general was detained in a hotel room. Although the Red Guards were on duty in the street outside, it was Kornilov's own loyal troops who patrolled the corridors, making sure that no harm came to their leader. Every morning Kornilov would take the salute from his hotel window while his own regiments marched past outside.

Still, these were the last days of uncertainty. Everywhere the Bolsheviks were taking power, and, in December 1917, Kornilov disguised himself and fled to the south of Russia.

German peace fuels Red Army's opposition

Kornilov gathers rag-tag army in the south . . . Bolsheviks make peace with Germany and direct the efforts of the Red Army towards the force of Kornilov's rebels . . . Before the storming of Ekaterinodar, Kornilov's headquarters are shelled . . . The general is fatally wounded . . . The planned attack is abandoned . . . The civil war continues.

Word that Kornilov was in the south, and that he intended to continue the fight against the Germans and restore some kind of 'democratic' government spread throughout Russia. Some officers and soldiers made their way to join him there.

It was a rag-tag kind of army that eventually gathered together. There was little money and no one received any pay at first. Food was short and weapons scarce. Rifles had either to be bought—mostly from the Cossacks—or stolen. Elderly colonels commanded seventeen-year-old cadets and Kornilov's army numbered altogether not more than 5000.

Horses, too, were in short supply and many of the officers had to walk through the winter snows. The short, square figure of Kornilov trudged ahead of the column. Grey-faced and tired, a haversack slung over his shoulder, this was the once-sprightly figure that a few weeks earlier had been given that hero's reception in Moscow.

Plan to capture Ekaterinodar

The Bolsheviks were negotiating a peace treaty with the Germans, and their forces, which included many troops of the former Imperial Army, became free to turn their attention upon Kornilov and his rebels. Kornilov's hope now was to try to capture the important city of Ekaterinodar, which was not far from the shores of the Black Sea. It was an important road and rail centre.

Between him and the city were units of the Red Army and, an even more difficult obstacle, the Kuban river which was swollen by the thawing snows.

Kornilov, a haversack slung over his shoulder, marches at the head of his rag-tag army.

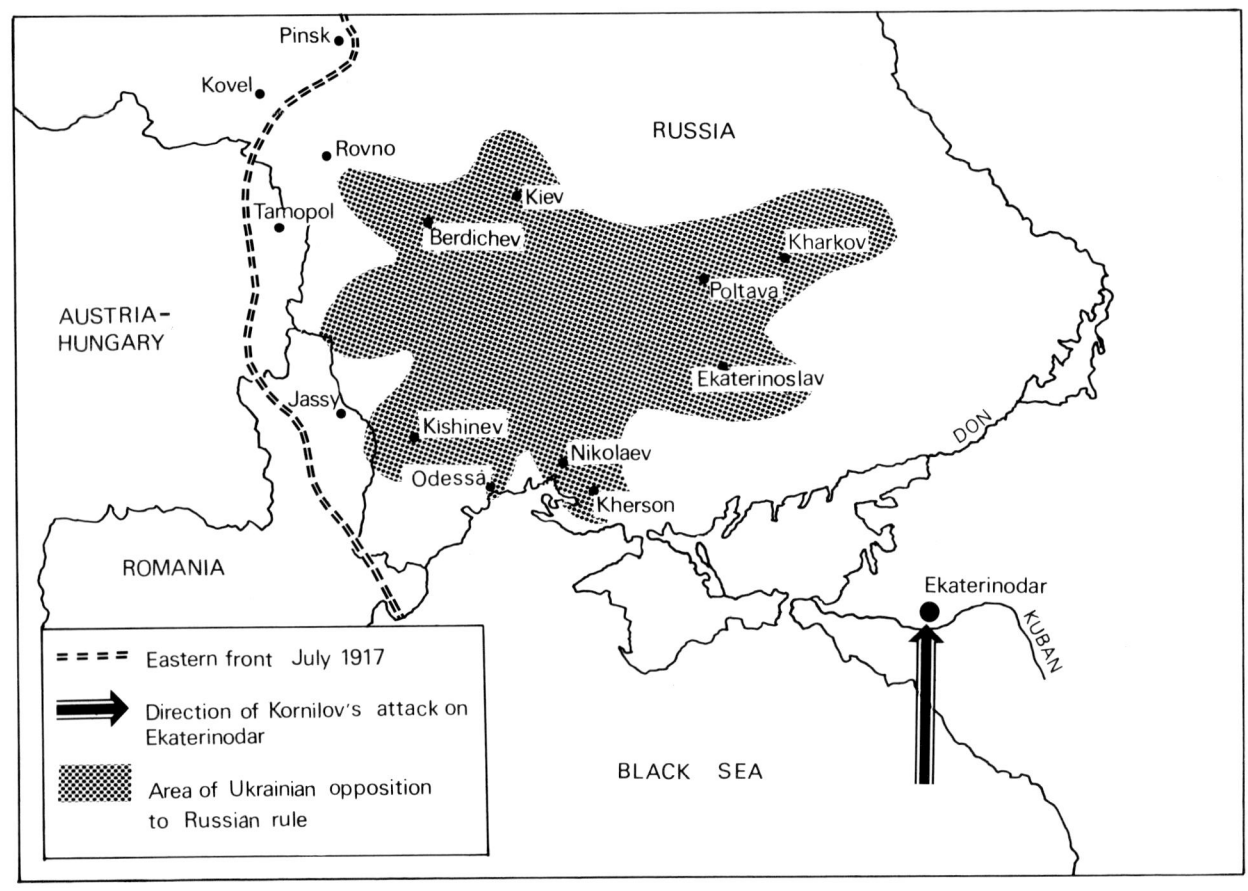

Kornilov's final hope of victory over the Bolsheviks was to seize the important city of Ekaterinodar.

Kornilov's men drove the Reds back towards the city. Then the general, who had lost none of his daring, ordered his troops across the river. It took three days by means of one ancient ferry which bucked perilously in the swiftly-flowing torrent. At last the way was clear for an attack on the city itself.

Above the town, overlooking its golden domes, rose a hill. On it stood a white-washed farmhouse, which Kornilov chose as his headquarters.

The spring sunshine shone weakly down upon the first wave of troops as they made their assault. The fighting was fierce and the commander of the Ekaterinodar garrison had been ordered to defend the city at all costs.

Russian fought Russian in a battle that was to

become typical of the bitter civil war. Kornilov's troops were beaten back and the defenders hastily erected more barricades. Then, one of Kornilov's commanders managed to bluff his way into the city with about 250 men.

Neither side wore particular uniforms, so it was often difficult to tell who was who, and in this case the attackers had removed any distinguishing marks from their clothing.

However they, too, were soon beaten back and withdrew. Kornilov decided that a massive frontal assault was the only way of capturing the city. Not all his officers agreed, because they knew this would result in terrible casualties. But none of them was prepared to oppose their determined leader, and the attack was planned for 14th April 1918.

Some of Kornilov's staff disagreed with their leader's tactics, but none of them openly opposed them.

This Red Army recruiting poster asks 'You, have you enrolled as a volunteer yet?'

Red soldiers on one of the armoured trains which engaged in bombardment throughout the civil war.

The farmhouse where Kornilov was staying was within range of the enemy artillery and occasionally shells whistled nearby. A number of times Kornilov's staff had tried to persuade him to withdraw out of range of the enemy guns. Typically, he refused. He wanted to be as close to the action as he could be.

On the morning before the attack, he was in his HQ when a shell landed on the farmhouse. Kornilov was in his room and, when his staff rushed in, they found him lying on the floor, wounded in the temple. Within a few minutes he was dead.

Civil war continues

The planned attack was abandoned, but Kornilov's death did not end the civil war. On the contrary the fighting went on for many months, almost to the end of 1920. Many thousands died, and the struggle that Kornilov had led at the start was always a hopeless one.

The revolt he began served only to unite the Bolsheviks. It helped Trotsky to set up the mighty Red Army, and established the Bolsheviks firmly in power in Russia.

Kornilov's part in the Russian revolution was much more that of a soldier than of a politician, and it was as a soldier that the man died.

Of those involved in the making of the Russian Revolution, Kornilov was perhaps the most sincere. Foolish he may have been, but he had been brought up as a soldier and he had acted—and died—like one.

As we have seen, the great movement begun by Lenin in the name of 'socialist democracy' turned into a terrible tyranny in which there was no freedom for Russian people to express their political beliefs or to choose their rulers. It is sad to think that so many gave their minds—and their lives—for an idea of freedom that was never to be achieved.

Dates and events

1870 Kornilov is born the son of a Cossack officer.
1898 First Congress of the Russian Social Democratic Party is held.
1904 Outbreak of war between Russia and Japan. Kornilov gains a distinguished war record.
1905 'Bloody Sunday'. Lenin returns from Switzerland to St. Petersburg.
1906 Russia's first elected parliament.
1914 The Great War is declared. Kornilov commands a brigade on the Carpathian front.
1917 Kornilov attends the State Conference in Moscow. Unsuccessful attempt to take Petrograd. Kerensky has Kornilov arrested. Disguised, Kornilov flees to the south of Russia. The Bolsheviks negotiate peace with the Germans. Lenin dismisses elected parliament.
1918 Kornilov's army attempt to take the city of Ekaterinodar. The morning before the attack, Kornilov is killed when a shell hits his headquarters.
1920 The civil war ends.

Glossary

Anarchist A person who seeks to abolish government and base society on voluntary cooperation.
Assassination The murder of a public or political figure by a surprise attack.
Bureaucracy Government by officials responsible only to their department chiefs.
Bolshevik Member of the Russian Majority—or extreme—Socialist party.
Capitalism Economic system based on the private ownership of the means of production, distribution and exchange.
Communism A society in which private ownership has been abolished and the means of production, distribution and exchange belong to the community.
Democracy Government by the people or their elected representatives.
Dictatorship Government by a ruler who is not restricted by a constitution, laws or recognized opposition.
Industrialization The development of industry on a large scale.
Liberal A person whose political views favour progress and reform.
Loyalist A patriotic supporter of his government or sovereign.
Marseillaise The French national anthem originally composed as a revolutionary song.
Menshevik Member of the moderate wing of the Russian Social Democratic Party, literally 'minority'.
Propaganda The organized spreading of information to assist or to damage the cause of a government or movement.
Provisional Government A government set up to meet the needs of an extraordinary situation on the understanding that it will be changed later.
Regime A system of government or a particular administration.
Soviet A local revolutionary council.
Socialism An economic system in which the means of production, distribution and exchange are owned by the community, usually through the state.

Further reading

The Russian Revolution by Robert Goldston (Bobbs Merrill, 1966)
Russia in Revolution by E. M. Halliday and Cyril E. Black (American Heritage, 1967)
Ten Days that Shook the World edited by John Reed (Random House, 1960)
Doomsday: 1917 The Destruction of Russia's Ruling Class by Douglas Brown (G. P. Putnam's Sons, 1976)
The Bolshevik Revolution 1917-1923 by Edward H. Carr (Macmillan, 1952)
Russia of the Tsars and Poets by S. A. Wilde (Chris Mass, 1976)
Lenin by Nina B. Baker (Vanguard, 1945)
Lenin and Trotsky by CBS News Staff (Franklin Watts, 1967)
Lenin and the Russian Revolution by Christopher Hill (Penguin, 1978)
Catastrophe: Kerensky's Own Story of the Russian Revolution by Alexander Kerenskey (Kraus Reprints, reprint of 1927 edition)

Index

Alma Ata, Trotsky in 28
Aurora 45

'Bloody Sunday' 10
Bolshevik party, formation of 10
Brussels meeting of Social Democratic Party 10

China, Kornilov in 52
Constantinople, Trotsky in 28
Cossacks 42, 56

Das Kapital 6
Davidovitch, Leon (Trotsky) 21
Democratic Assembly 24

Ekaterinodar, plan to capture 56

Finland, Lenin in 16
France, Lenin in 7

Geneva, Lenin in 11
Germany, Lenin in 7
   Lenin's return from 14
Great War, the 13, 41, 52

Ilyich, the 28
Imperial Army, the 56
Industrialization of Russia 5

Iskra (The Spark) 9

Japan, war between Russia and 10, 52

Kamenev, Lev Borisovich 26
Kerensky, Alexander **37-49**, 52, 55
Kornilov, Lavr Georgevitch **51-61**

Labour camps 31
Lenin, Vladimir Ilyich **5-19**, 21, 24, 25, 33, 37, 46, 61
London, Lenin in 9

Marx, Karl 6
Menshevik party, formation of 10
Mexico, Trotsky in 31-4
Mornard, Jacson 33-4
Munich, Lenin in 9

New York, Trotsky in 21
Norway, Trotsky in 31
Nova Scotia, Trotsky in 21

Peace Treaty with Germany 18, 56
Provisional Government 13, 15, 16, 37, 39, 41, 42, 46, 47, 52

Red Army 22, 24, 56, 60

Red Guards 23, 41, 42, 44, 45, 47, 54, 55
Riga, fall of 44

Savage Division 54
Second World War 34
Secret police 5, 21, 26, 31, 34
Sedov, Leon 32-3
Sedov, Sergey 32
Simbirsk 5, 37
Social Democratic Party 10, 13
South Russian Workers' Union 21
Soviet, the 39, 41, 42
Stalin, Joseph 26, 30, 31, 34
State Conference, the 42, 52, 54
Switzerland, Lenin in 7, 14

Tekintzy regiment 53
Trials, Stalin's show 31
Trotsky, Leon 10, **21-34**, 37, 46, 47, 60
Tsar Nicholas II 5, 8, 10, 11, 12, 13, 14, 19, 51

Ulyanov, Vladimir Ilyich (Lenin) 5

Winter Palace 10, 47

Zinoviev, Grigori Evseevich 26

Picture acknowledgements

The publishers would like to thank all those who provided the pictures which illustrate this book on the following pages: BBC Hulton Picture Library 49, 61; Mike Bishop 20, 22, 23, 32; David King Collection 10, 18, 24, 25, 28, 30, 31, 39, 42, 48, 53, 54, 59, 60 (below); John Topham Picture Library 34, 35; Mansell Collection 6, 38, 44, 52; Novosti Press Agency *front cover* 4, 7, 12, 13, 16, 17, 43; Popperfoto 27; Dan Woods 9, 11, 36, 40, 46, 51, 55, 57.